SAVING ANIMALS FROM THE BRINK

SAVING THE SILVERTIP

GRIZZLY BEAR COMEBACK

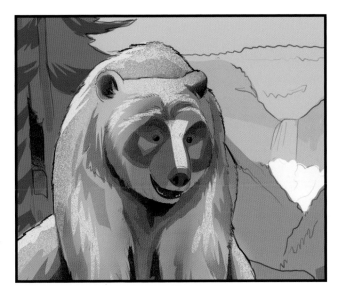

BY TIM COOKE
ILLUSTRATED BY EDU COLL

BEARPORT PUBLISHING
Minneapolis, Minnesota

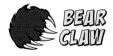

BEAR CLAW

Credits: 20, © Volodymyr Burdiak/Shutterstock; 21, © Scott E Read/Shutterstock; 22t, © Vaclav Sebek/Shutterstock; 22b, © Yatra/Shutterstock.

Editor: Sarah Eason
Proofreader: Harriet McGregor
Designers: Jessica Moon and Steve Mead
Picture Researcher: Rachel Blount

DISCLAIMER: This graphic story is a dramatization based on true events. It is intended to give the reader a sense of the narrative rather than a presentation of actual details as they occurred.

Library of Congress Cataloging-in-Publication Data

Names: Cooke, Tim, 1961- author. | Coll, Edu, 1996- illustrator.
Title: Saving the silvertip : grizzly bear comeback / by Tim Cooke ;
  illustrated by Edu Coll.
Description: Bear claw books edition. | Minneapolis, Minnesota : Bearport
  Publishing Company, [2022] | Series: Saving animals from the brink |
  Includes bibliographical references and index.
Identifiers: LCCN 2020057410 (print) | LCCN 2020057411 (ebook) | ISBN
  9781636910475 (library binding) | ISBN 9781636910543 (paperback) | ISBN
  9781636910611 (ebook)
Subjects: LCSH: Craighead, John J. (John Johnson), 1916-2016--Juvenile
  literature. | Craighead, Frank C., Jr. (Frank Cooper),
  1916-2001--Juvenile literature. | Conservationists--United
  States--Biography--Juvenile literature. | Naturalists--United
  States--Biography--Juvenile literature. | Grizzly
  bear--Conservation--Yellowstone National Park. | Endangered
  species--Conservation--Yellowstone National Park.
Classification: LCC QL737.C27 C664 2022 (print) | LCC QL737.C27 (ebook) |
  DDC 639.97/97840978752--dc23
LC record available at https://lccn.loc.gov/2020057410
LC ebook record available at https://lccn.loc.gov/2020057411

For more information, write to Bearport Publishing, 5357 Penn Avenue South, Minneapolis, MN 55419. Printed in the United States of America.

CONTENTS

CHAPTER 1

A GRIZZLY ENCOUNTER

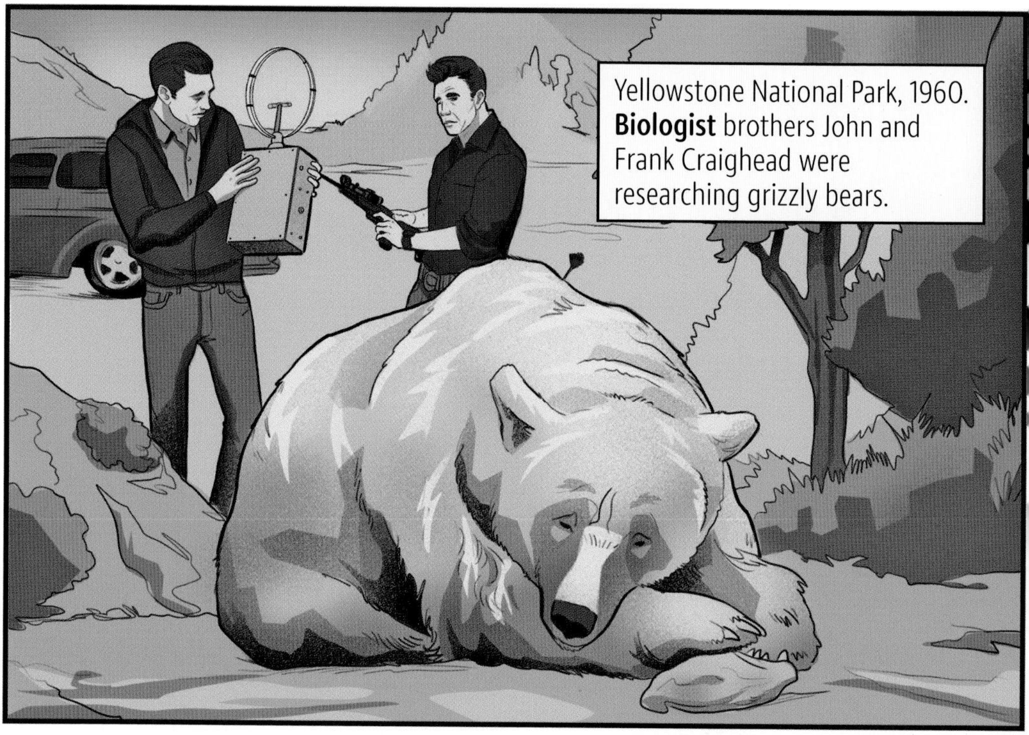
Yellowstone National Park, 1960. **Biologist** brothers John and Frank Craighead were researching grizzly bears.

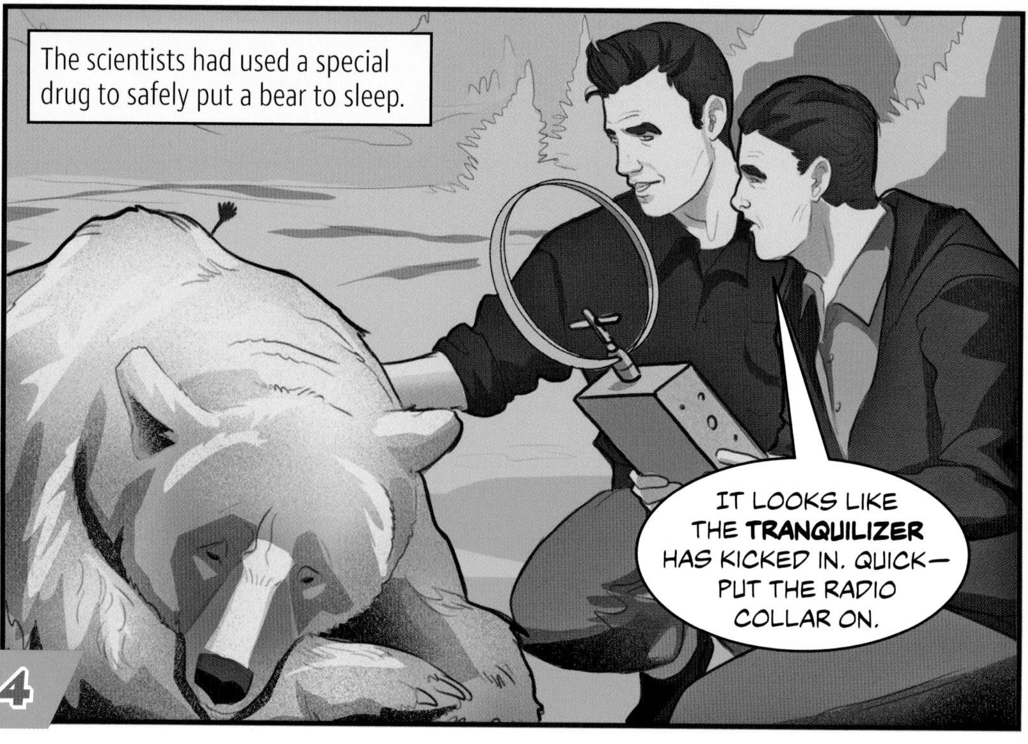
The scientists had used a special drug to safely put a bear to sleep.
IT LOOKS LIKE THE **TRANQUILIZER** HAS KICKED IN. QUICK—PUT THE RADIO COLLAR ON.

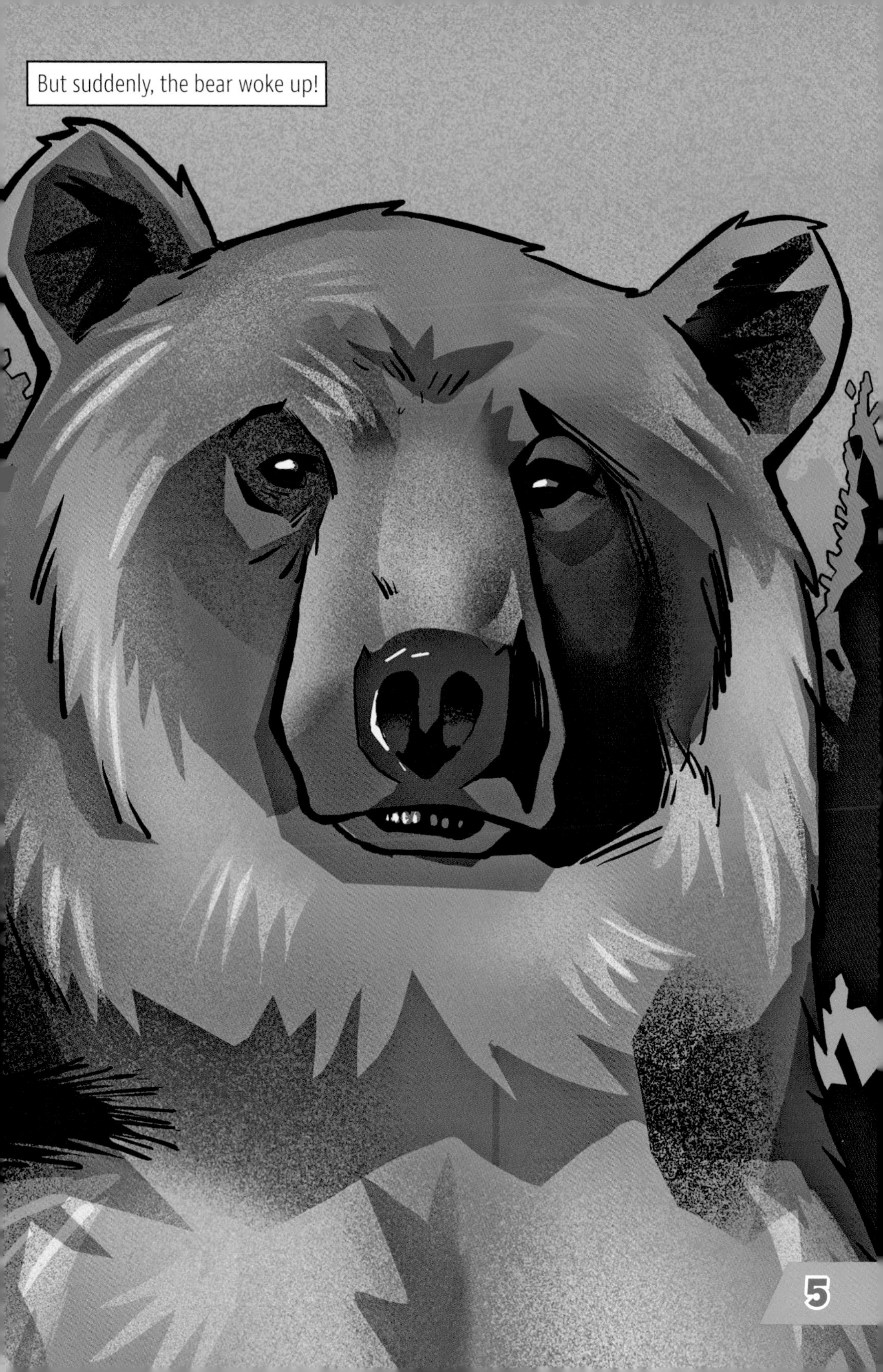
But suddenly, the bear woke up!

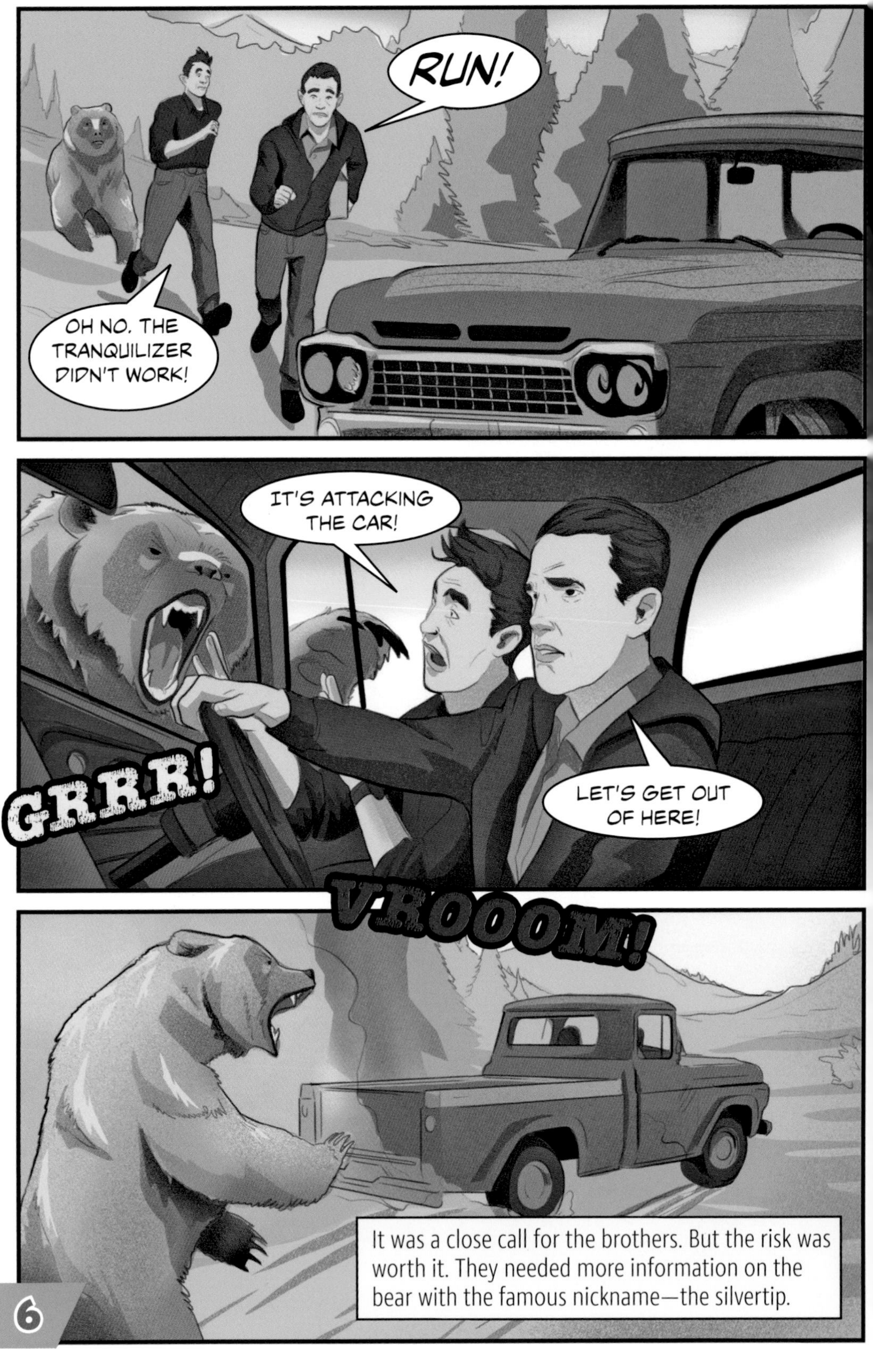
RUN!
OH NO. THE TRANQUILIZER DIDN'T WORK!
IT'S ATTACKING THE CAR!
LET'S GET OUT OF HERE!
GRRR!
VROOOOM!
It was a close call for the brothers. But the risk was worth it. They needed more information on the bear with the famous nickname—the silvertip.

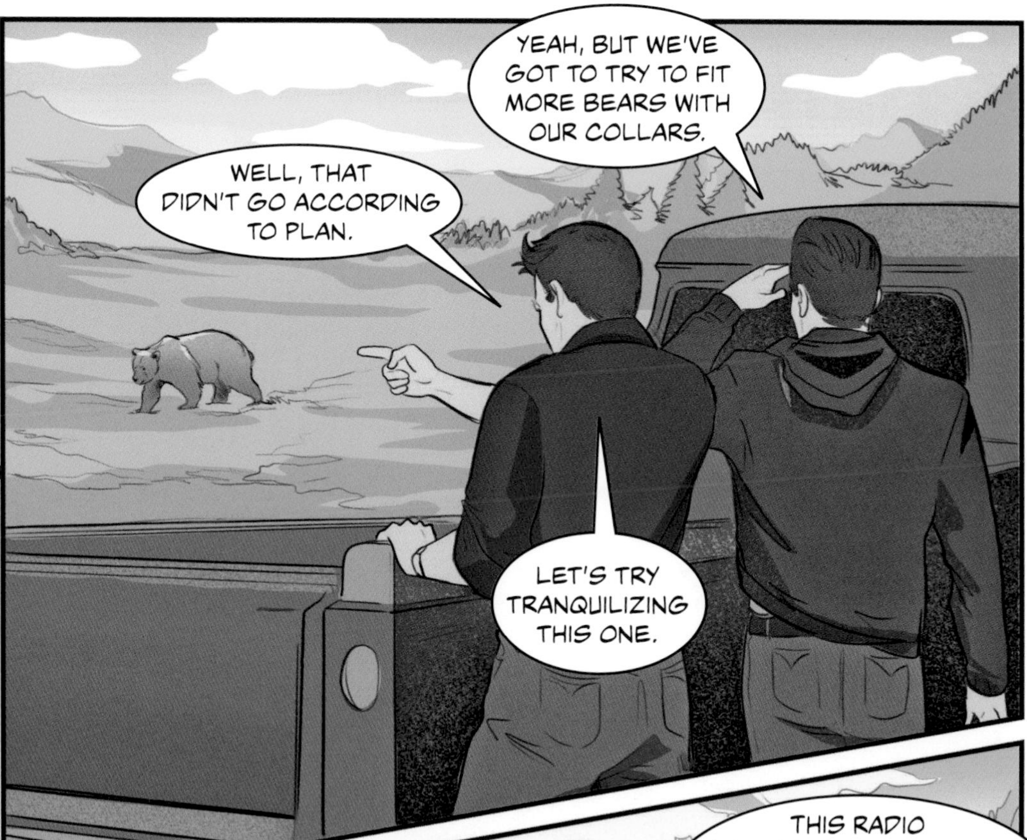
WELL, THAT DIDN'T GO ACCORDING TO PLAN.
YEAH, BUT WE'VE GOT TO TRY TO FIT MORE BEARS WITH OUR COLLARS.
LET'S TRY TRANQUILIZING THIS ONE.

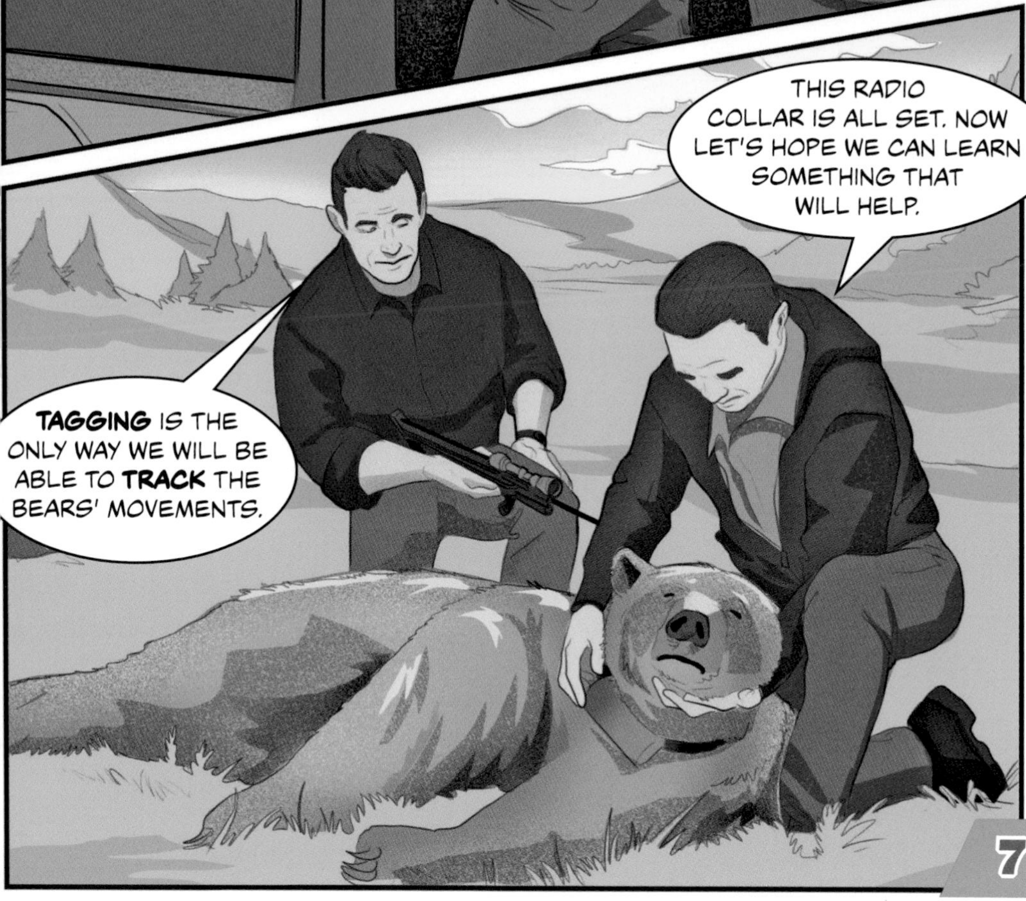
THIS RADIO COLLAR IS ALL SET. NOW LET'S HOPE WE CAN LEARN SOMETHING THAT WILL HELP.
TAGGING IS THE ONLY WAY WE WILL BE ABLE TO **TRACK** THE BEARS' MOVEMENTS.

CHAPTER 2

STUDYING THE BEARS

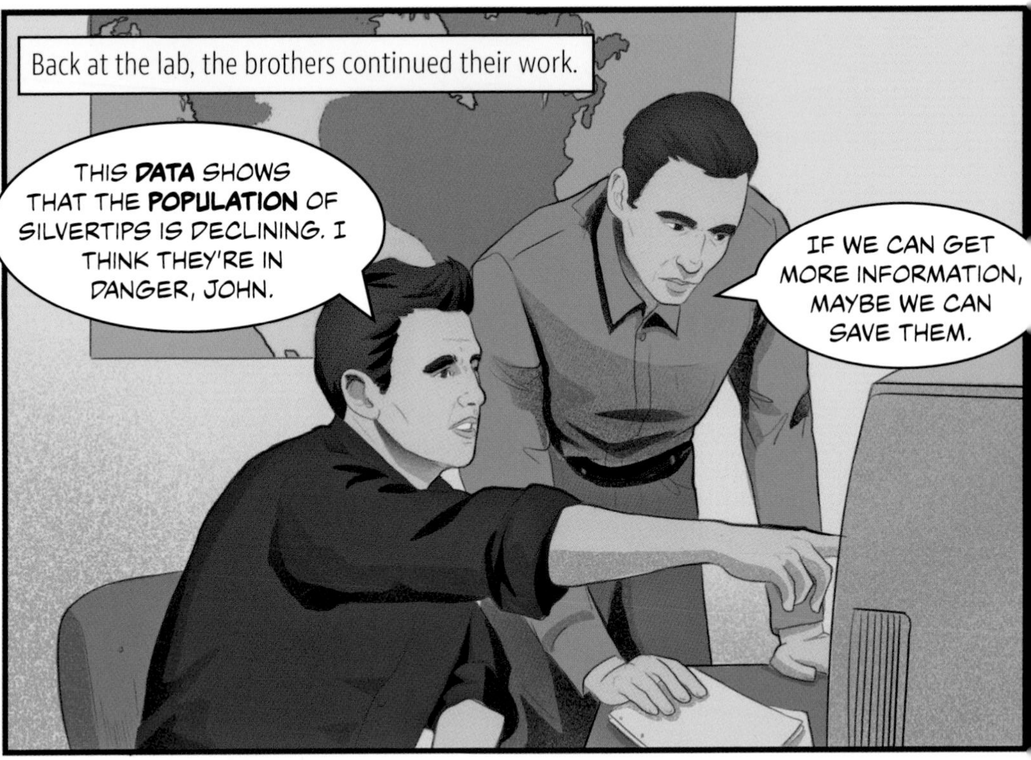
Back at the lab, the brothers continued their work.
THIS DATA SHOWS THAT THE POPULATION OF SILVERTIPS IS DECLINING. I THINK THEY'RE IN DANGER, JOHN.
IF WE CAN GET MORE INFORMATION, MAYBE WE CAN SAVE THEM.

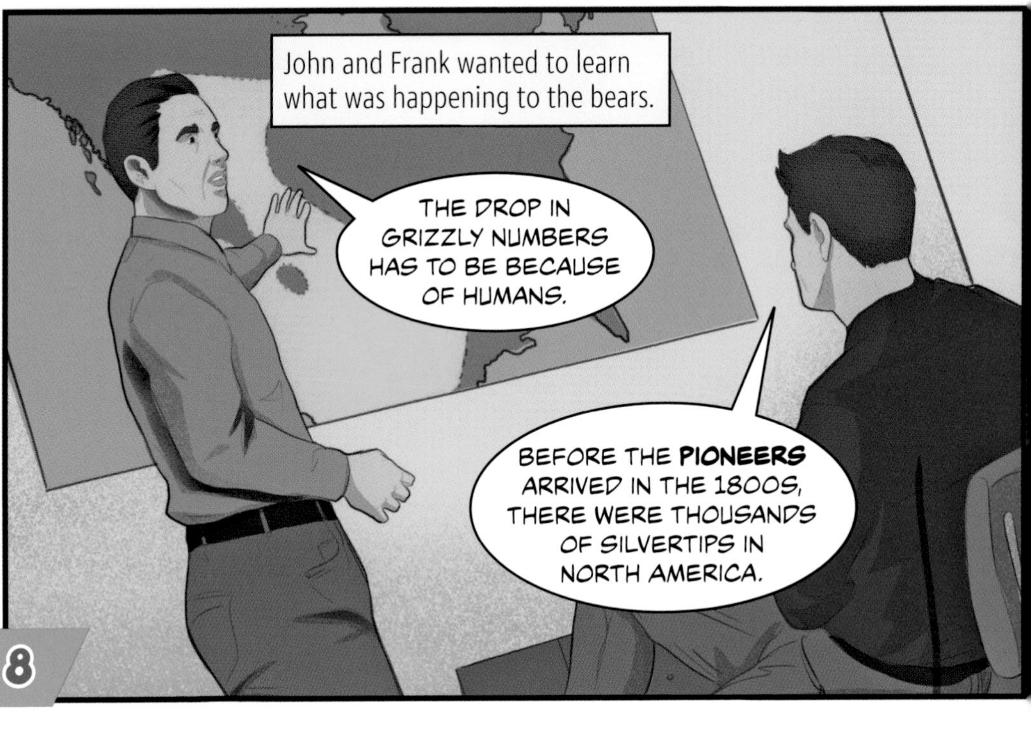
John and Frank wanted to learn what was happening to the bears.
THE DROP IN GRIZZLY NUMBERS HAS TO BE BECAUSE OF HUMANS.
BEFORE THE PIONEERS ARRIVED IN THE 1800S, THERE WERE THOUSANDS OF SILVERTIPS IN NORTH AMERICA.

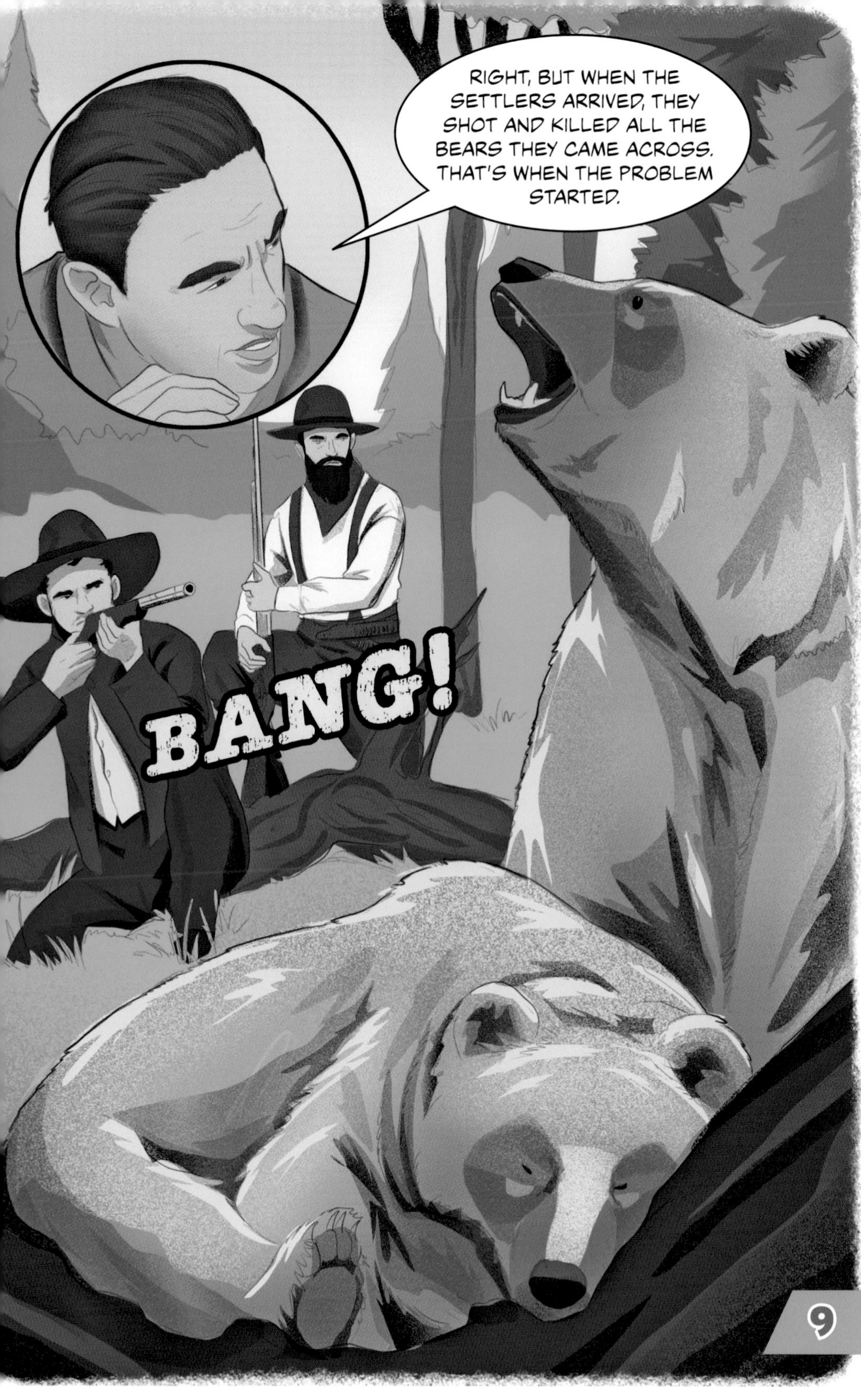
RIGHT, BUT WHEN THE SETTLERS ARRIVED, THEY SHOT AND KILLED ALL THE BEARS THEY CAME ACROSS. THAT'S WHEN THE PROBLEM STARTED.
BANG!

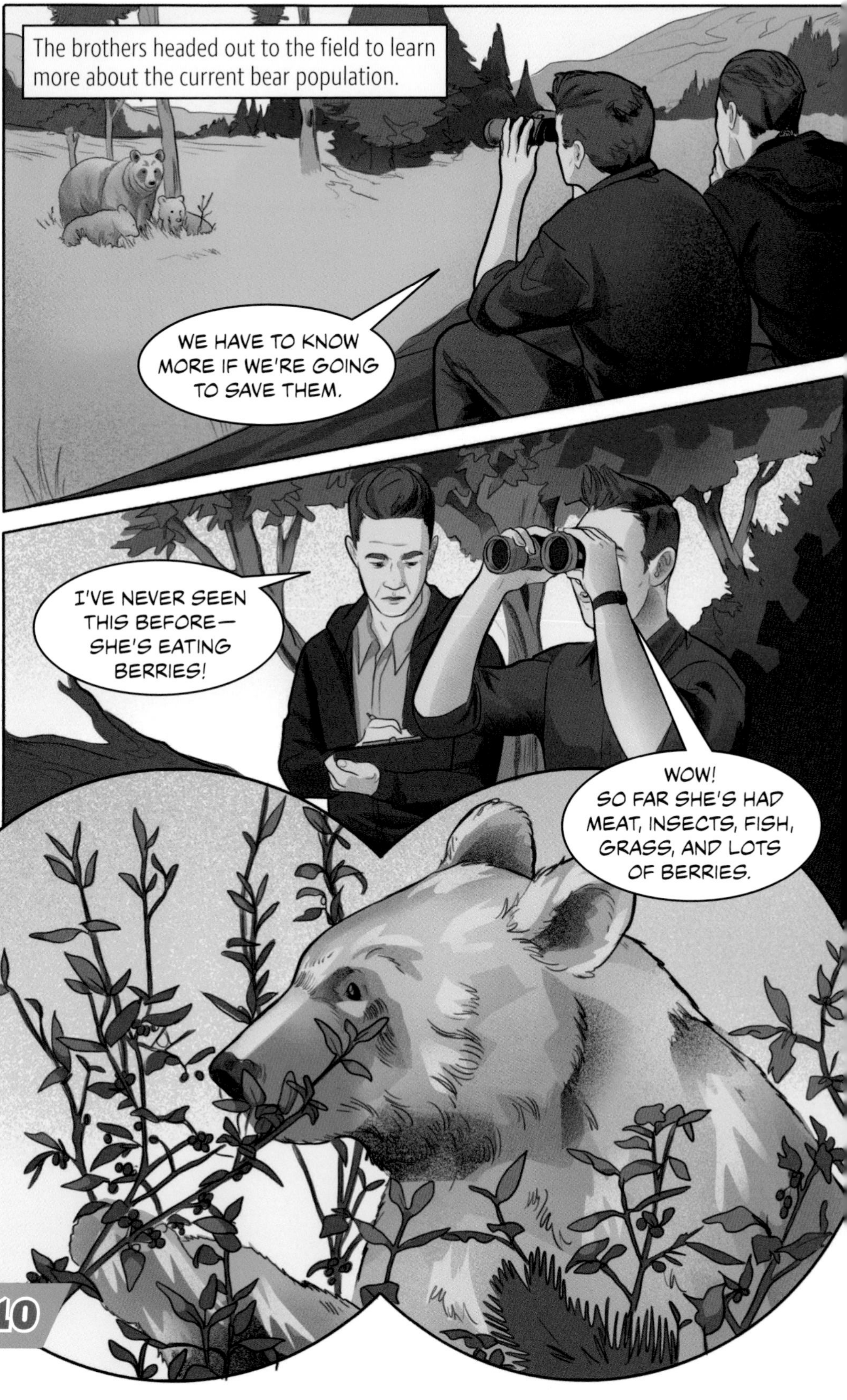
The brothers headed out to the field to learn more about the current bear population.
WE HAVE TO KNOW MORE IF WE'RE GOING TO SAVE THEM.
I'VE NEVER SEEN THIS BEFORE— SHE'S EATING BERRIES!
WOW! SO FAR SHE'S HAD MEAT, INSECTS, FISH, GRASS, AND LOTS OF BERRIES.

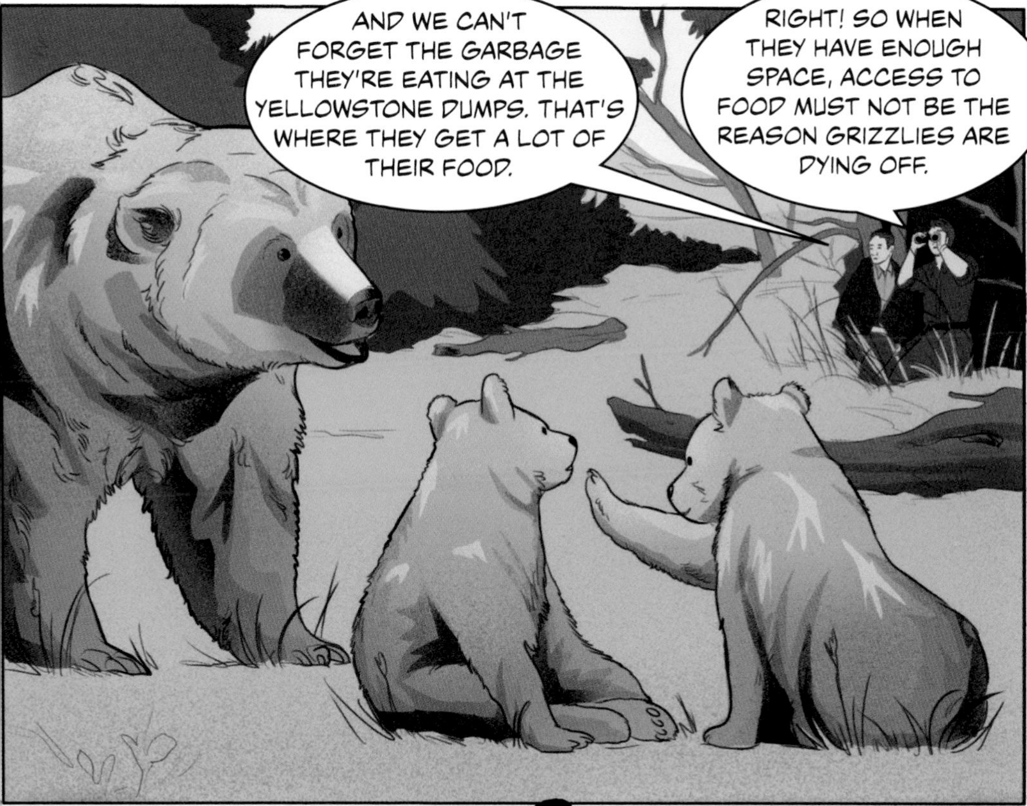
AND WE CAN'T FORGET THE GARBAGE THEY'RE EATING AT THE YELLOWSTONE DUMPS. THAT'S WHERE THEY GET A LOT OF THEIR FOOD.
RIGHT! SO WHEN THEY HAVE ENOUGH SPACE, ACCESS TO FOOD MUST NOT BE THE REASON GRIZZLIES ARE DYING OFF.

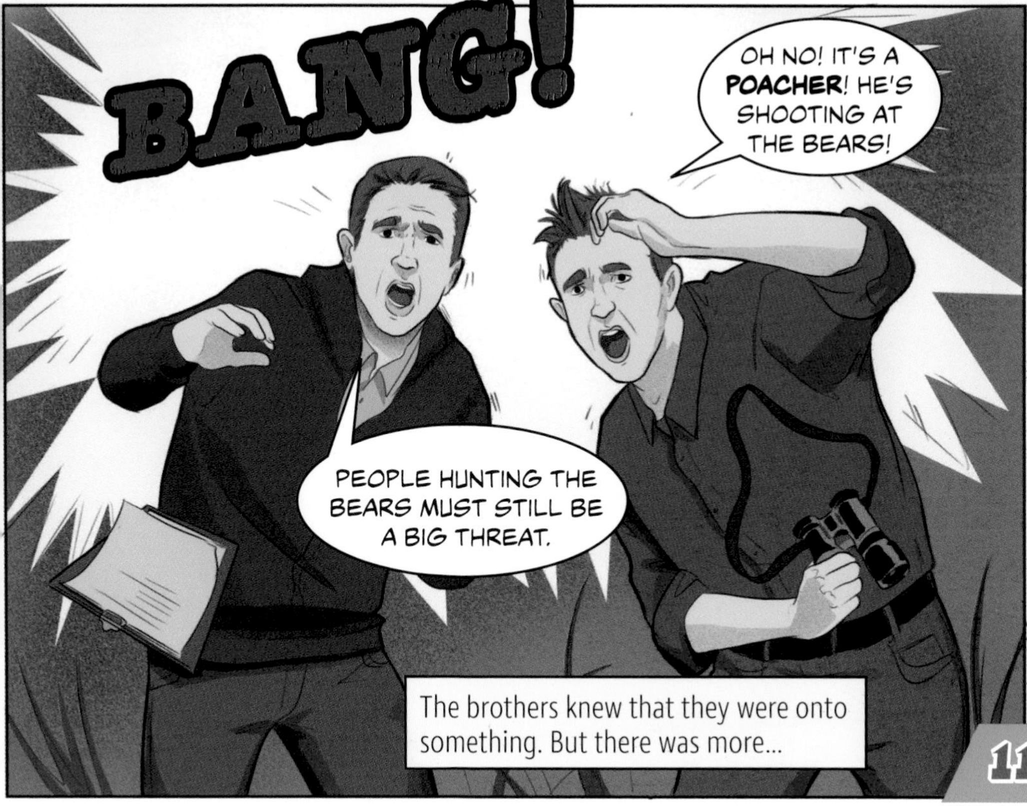
BANG!
PEOPLE HUNTING THE BEARS MUST STILL BE A BIG THREAT.
OH NO! IT'S A **POACHER**! HE'S SHOOTING AT THE BEARS!
The brothers knew that they were onto something. But there was more...

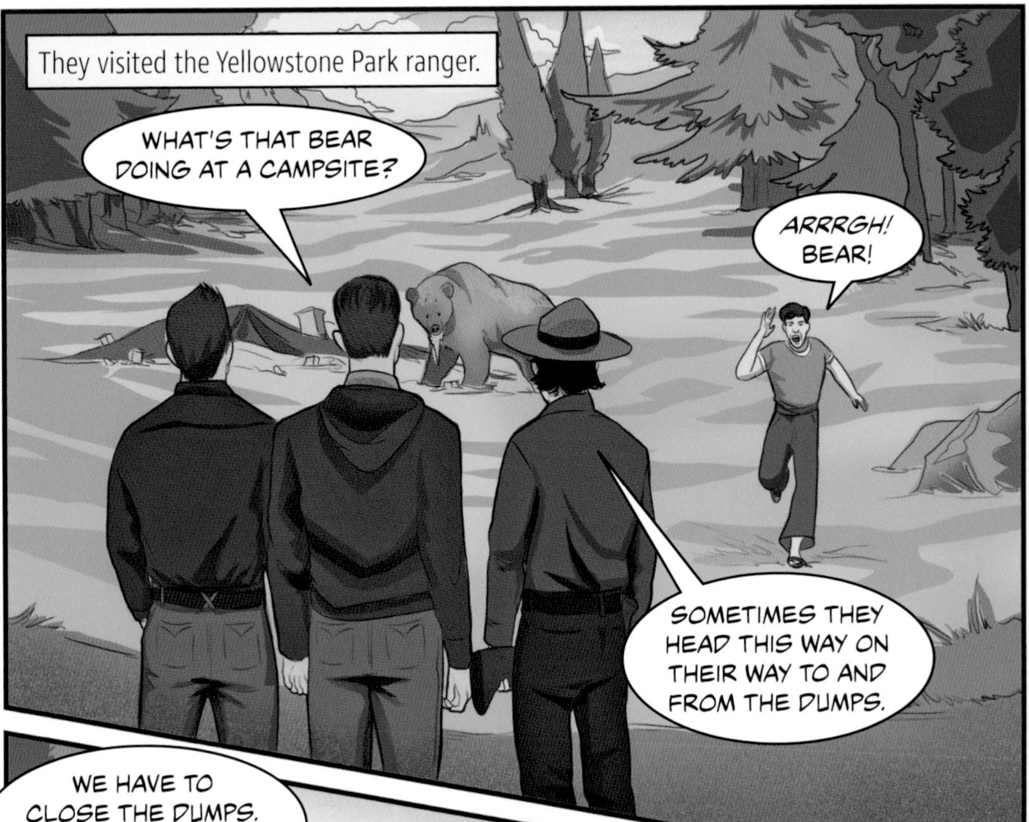
They visited the Yellowstone Park ranger.
WHAT'S THAT BEAR DOING AT A CAMPSITE?
ARRRGH! BEAR!
SOMETIMES THEY HEAD THIS WAY ON THEIR WAY TO AND FROM THE DUMPS.

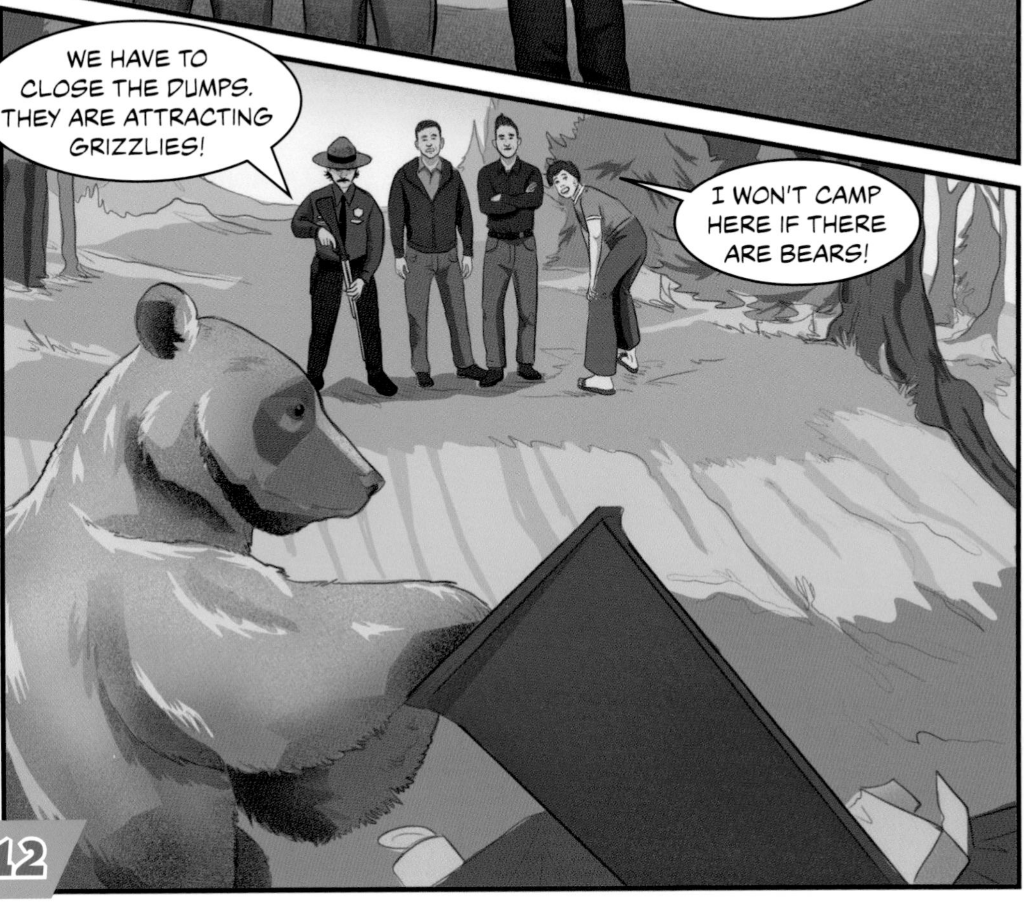
WE HAVE TO CLOSE THE DUMPS. THEY ARE ATTRACTING GRIZZLIES!
I WON'T CAMP HERE IF THERE ARE BEARS!

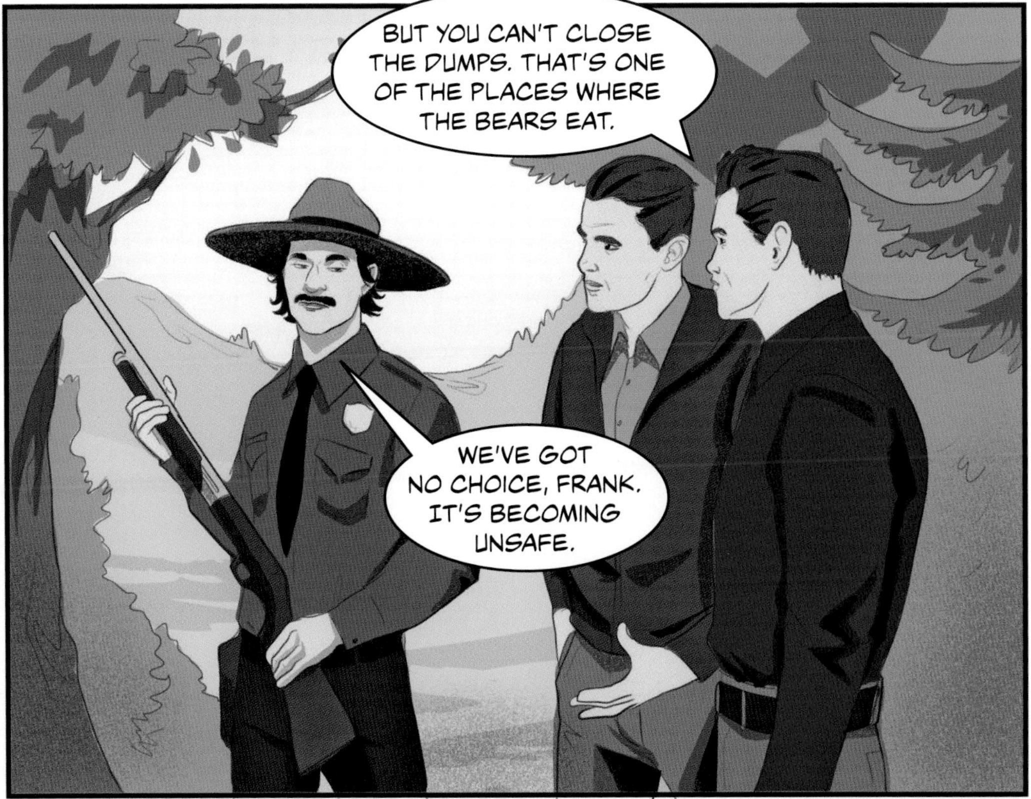
BUT YOU CAN'T CLOSE THE DUMPS. THAT'S ONE OF THE PLACES WHERE THE BEARS EAT.
WE'VE GOT NO CHOICE, FRANK. IT'S BECOMING UNSAFE.

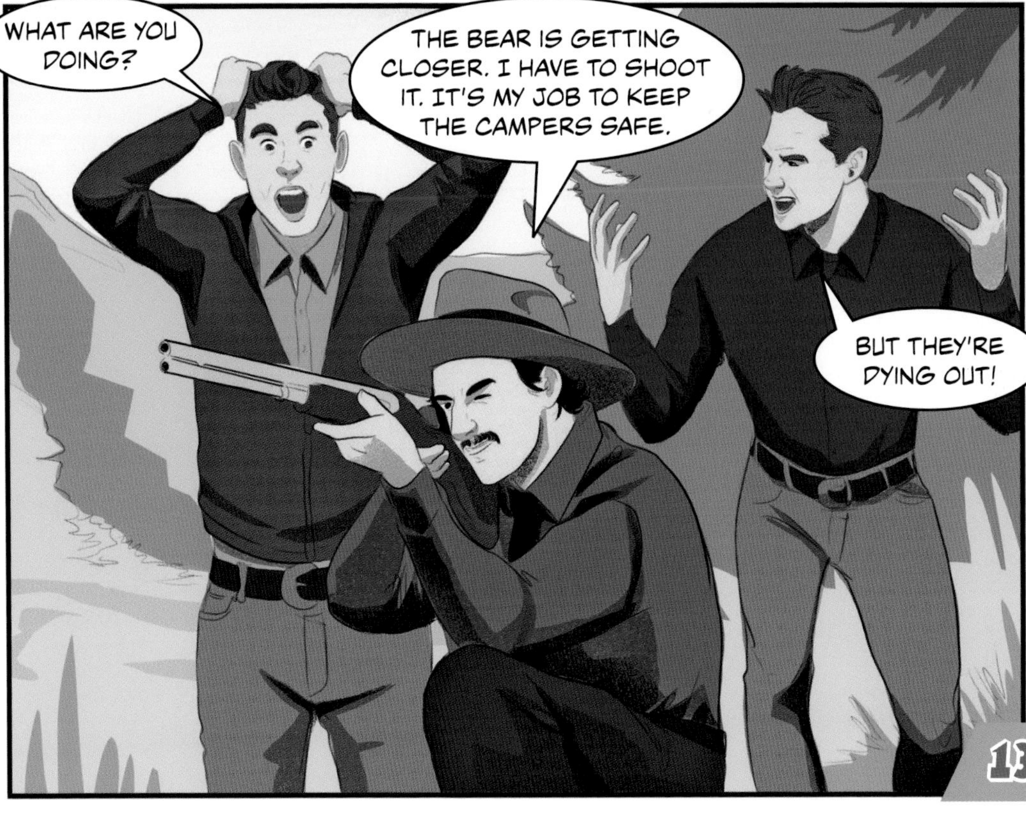
WHAT ARE YOU DOING?
THE BEAR IS GETTING CLOSER. I HAVE TO SHOOT IT. IT'S MY JOB TO KEEP THE CAMPERS SAFE.
BUT THEY'RE DYING OUT!

CHAPTER 3

PROTECTING THE SILVERTIP

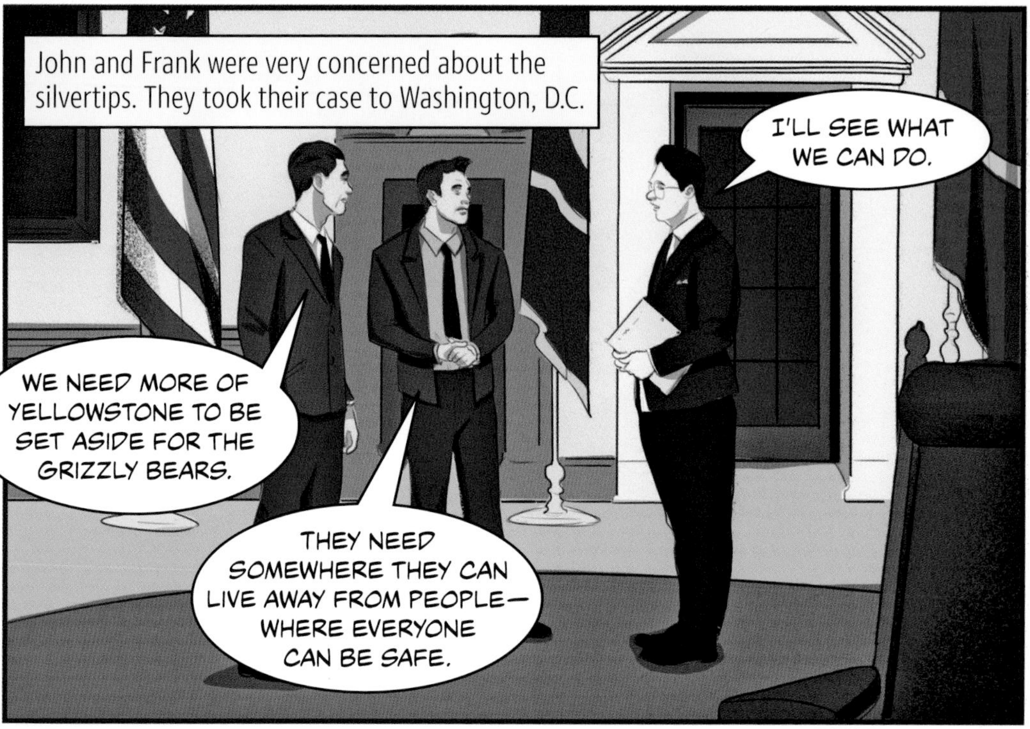
John and Frank were very concerned about the silvertips. They took their case to Washington, D.C.
I'LL SEE WHAT WE CAN DO.
WE NEED MORE OF YELLOWSTONE TO BE SET ASIDE FOR THE GRIZZLY BEARS.
THEY NEED SOMEWHERE THEY CAN LIVE AWAY FROM PEOPLE— WHERE EVERYONE CAN BE SAFE.

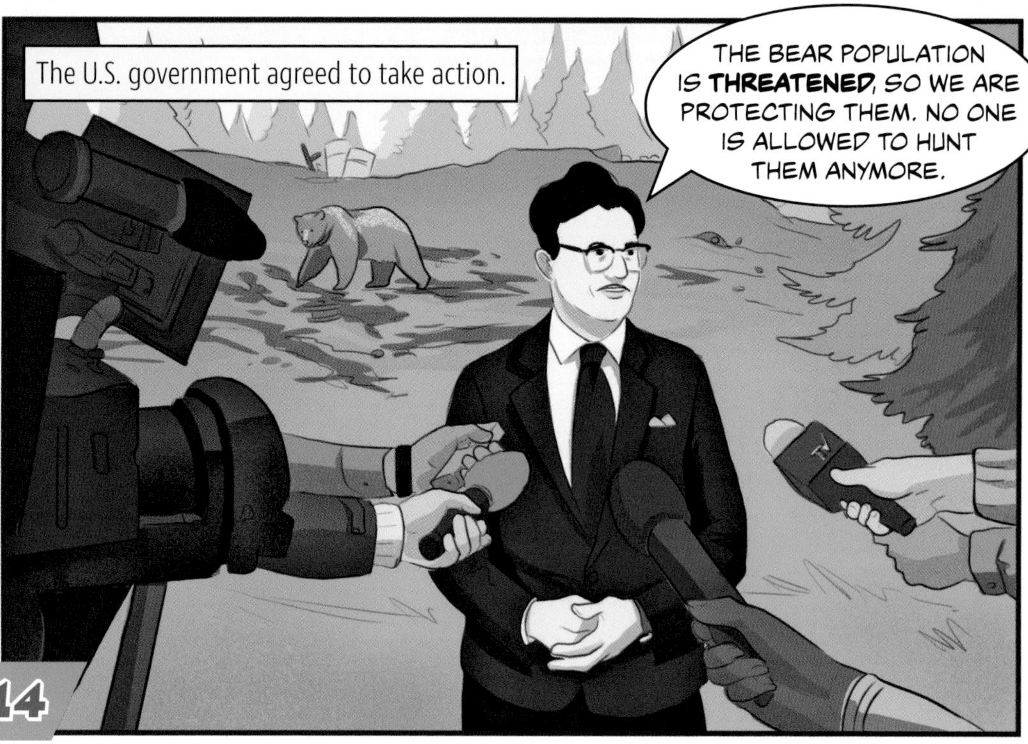
The U.S. government agreed to take action.
THE BEAR POPULATION IS **THREATENED**, SO WE ARE PROTECTING THEM. NO ONE IS ALLOWED TO HUNT THEM ANYMORE.

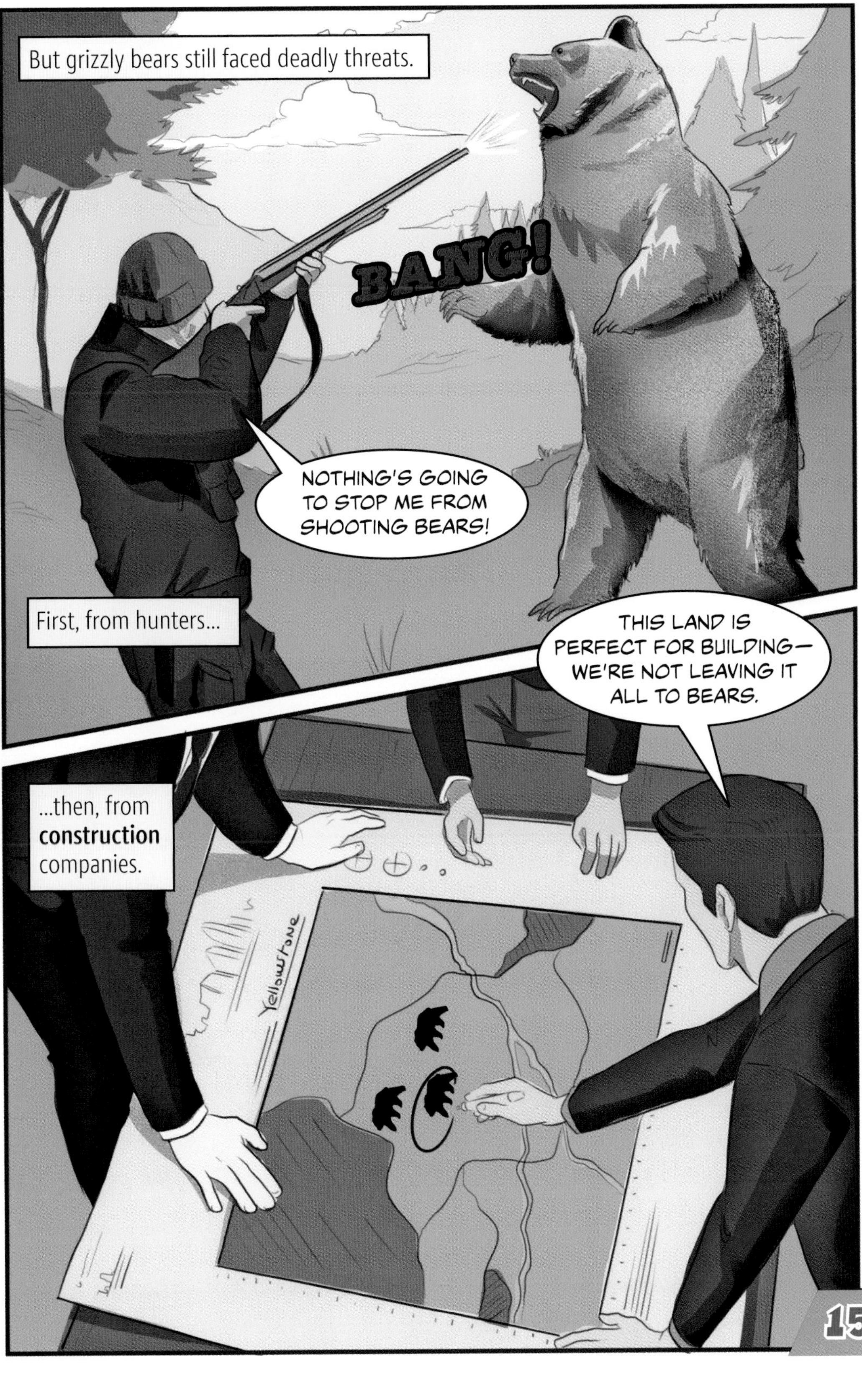

But grizzly bears still faced deadly threats.
BANG!
NOTHING'S GOING TO STOP ME FROM SHOOTING BEARS!
First, from hunters...
THIS LAND IS PERFECT FOR BUILDING—WE'RE NOT LEAVING IT ALL TO BEARS.
...then, from **construction** companies.
Yellowstone

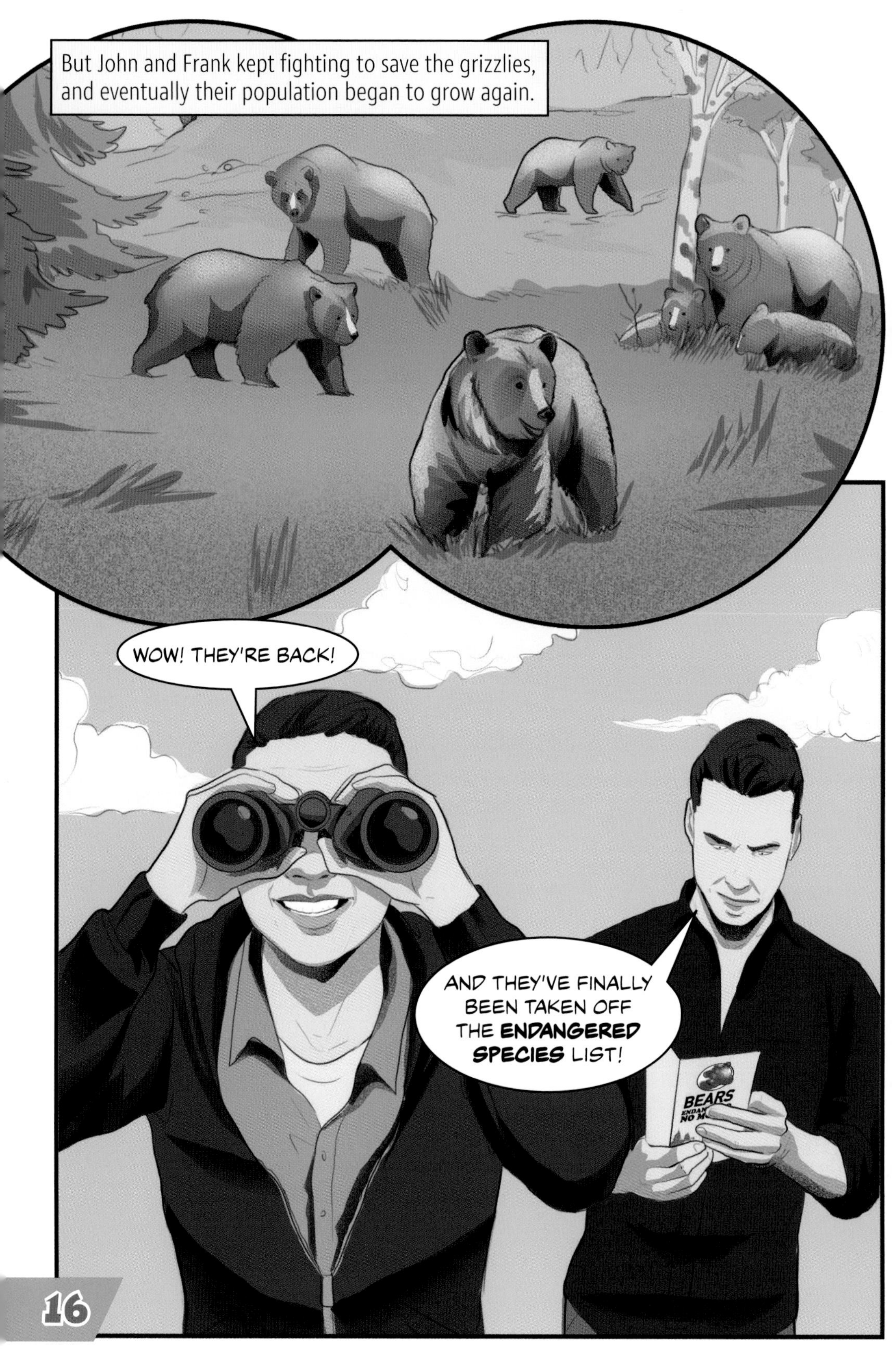
But John and Frank kept fighting to save the grizzlies, and eventually their population began to grow again.
WOW! THEY'RE BACK!
AND THEY'VE FINALLY BEEN TAKEN OFF THE **ENDANGERED SPECIES** LIST!
BEARS

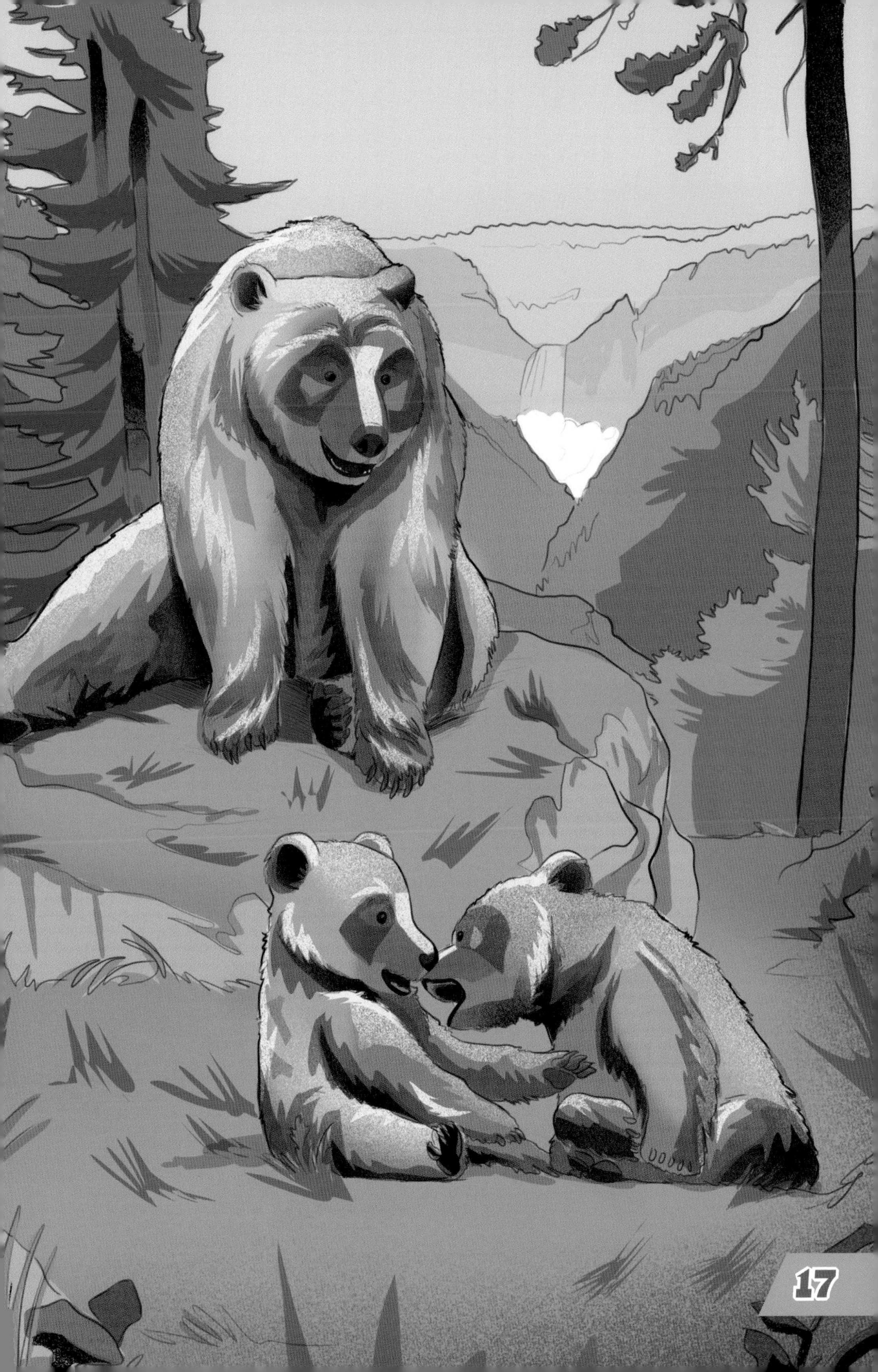

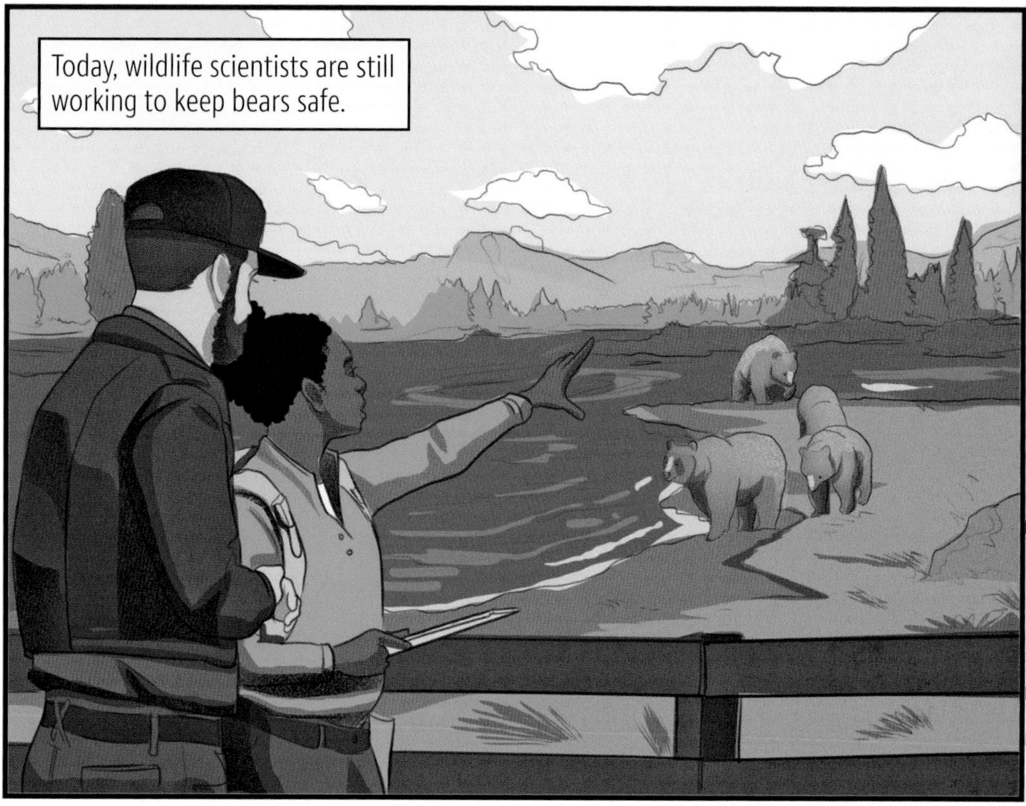
Today, wildlife scientists are still working to keep bears safe.

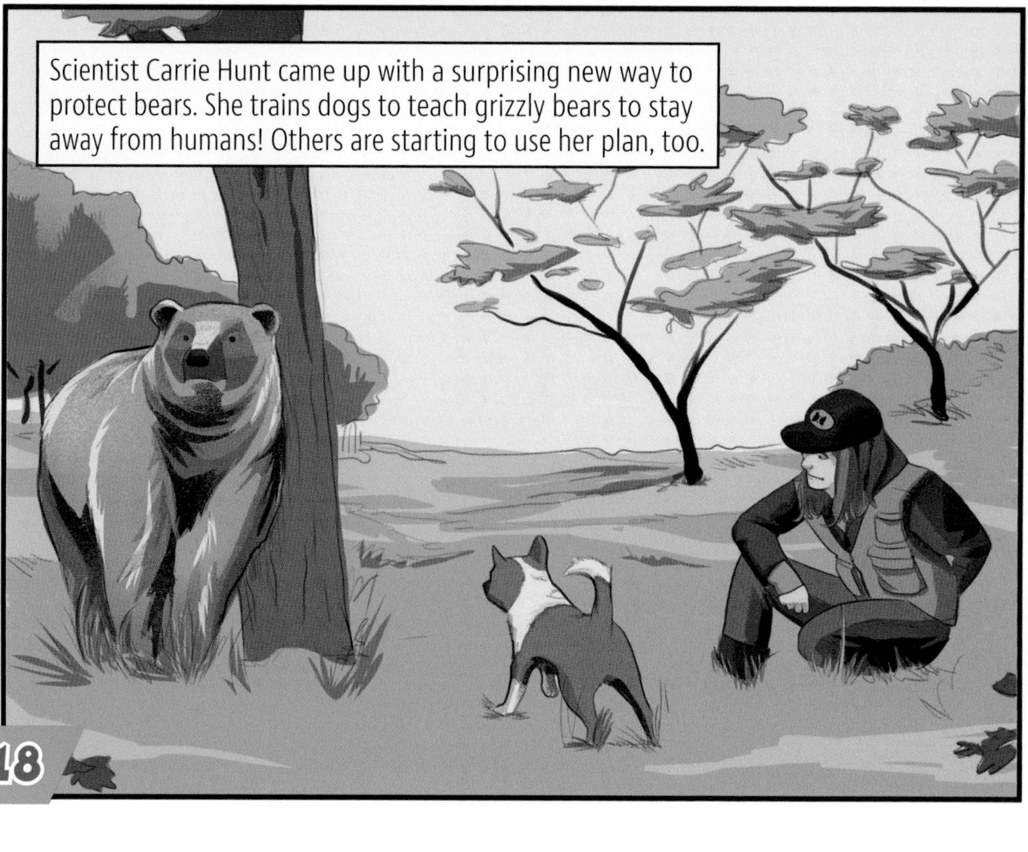
Scientist Carrie Hunt came up with a surprising new way to protect bears. She trains dogs to teach grizzly bears to stay away from humans! Others are starting to use her plan, too.

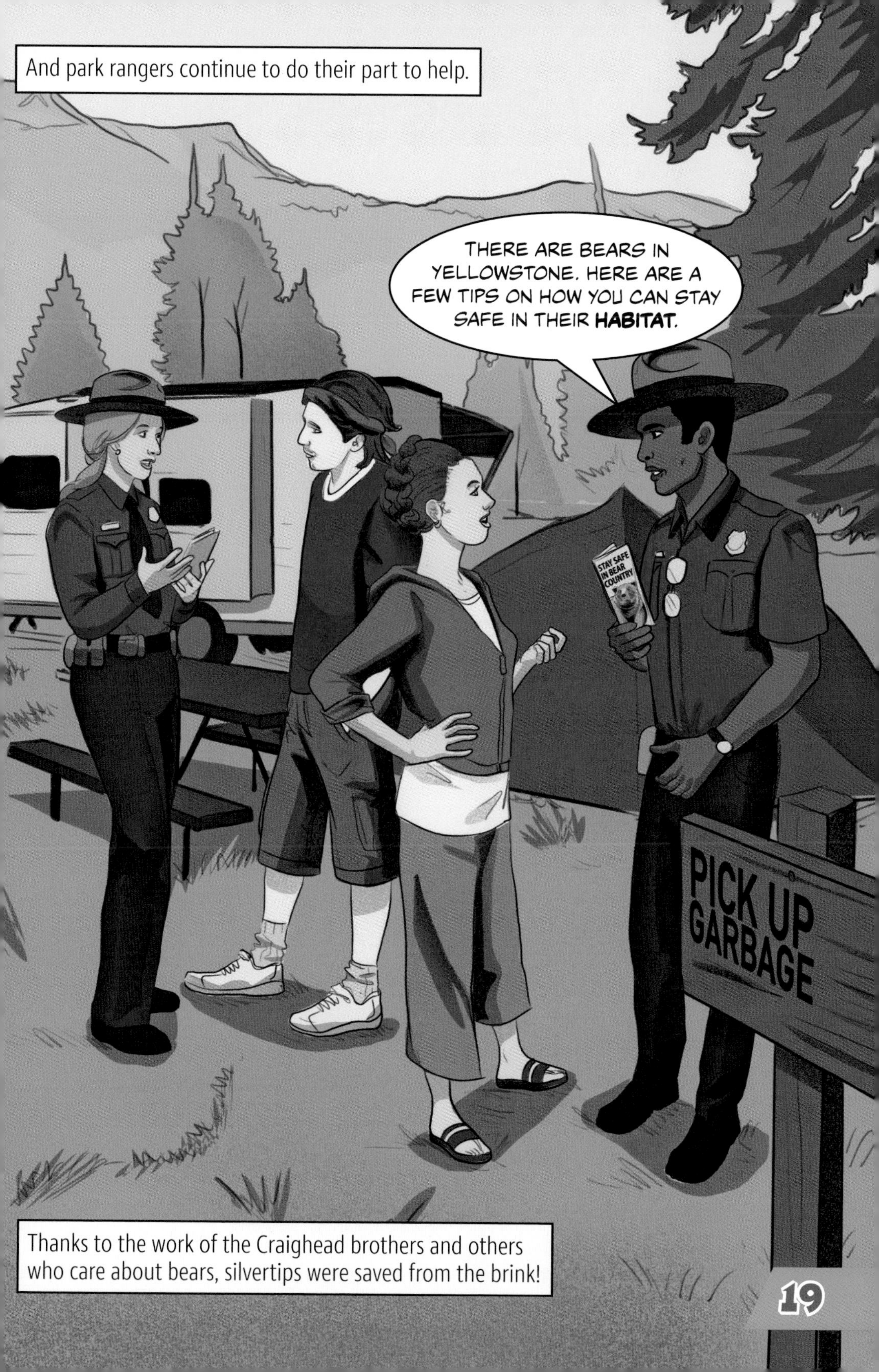
And park rangers continue to do their part to help.
THERE ARE BEARS IN YELLOWSTONE. HERE ARE A FEW TIPS ON HOW YOU CAN STAY SAFE IN THEIR **HABITAT**.
STAY SAFE IN BEAR COUNTRY
PICK UP GARBAGE
Thanks to the work of the Craighead brothers and others who care about bears, silvertips were saved from the brink!

GRIZZLY BEAR FACTS

In 1973, Congress passed the Endangered Species Act. This law protects animals and plants that are in danger of dying out in the United States. Harmful activities, such as hunting, capturing, or collecting endangered species, are **illegal** under this act.

MOST GRIZZLY BEARS LIVE FOR ABOUT 18 YEARS. SOME CAN LIVE INTO THEIR LATE 20S.

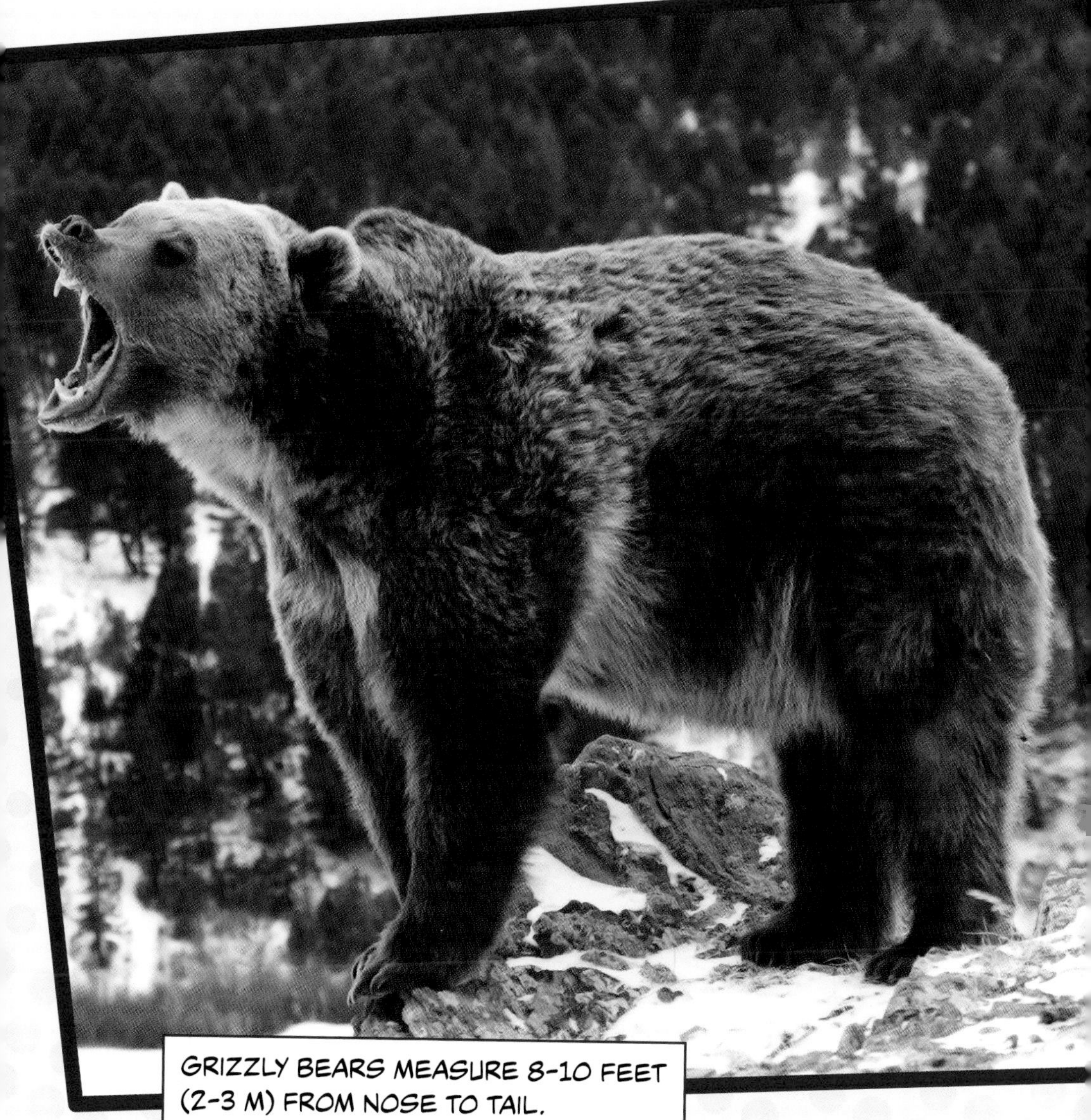

GRIZZLY BEARS MEASURE 8–10 FEET (2–3 M) FROM NOSE TO TAIL.

The grizzly bear was one of the first species listed under the Endangered Species Act. The grizzlies in Yellowstone National Park were listed as a threatened species in 1975.

In 1700, the grizzly bear population in North America was around 100,000. Today, the population in Alaska and Canada is about 50,000–55,000, and in the lower United States, it is between 1,000 and 1,500.

OTHER BEARS IN DANGER

Grizzly bears were saved from the brink, but other bears around the world are still struggling.

POLAR BEARS

Polar bears live along the shores of the Arctic Ocean. But they are in danger of disappearing due to loss of habitat. Many scientists believe their greatest danger is warmer temperatures and melting sea ice. Researchers are studying the effects of **climate change** on polar bears. They are looking for ways to save sea ice.

POLAR BEARS' WHITE FUR HELPS THEM BLEND IN WITH THEIR SNOWY HABITAT.

SCIENTISTS ARE **BREEDING** SUN BEARS AT SOME ZOOS TO INCREASE THEIR POPULATION.

SUN BEARS

Sun bears live in the forests of Asia in Borneo, Myanmar, Thailand, and the Malay Peninsula. They are the smallest bears in the world. Sun bears are thought to be dying out. No one knows how many are left in the wild. Hunting, capturing, and loss of habitat are decreasing their numbers. Many countries are trying to help by **banning** the sale of bear parts.

GLOSSARY

banning not allowing

biologist a scientist who studies plants or animals

breeding producing young

climate change the change of Earth's climate and weather patterns, including the warming of Earth's air and oceans, due to human activities

construction building

data facts and statistics

endangered species a group of animals in danger of dying out

habitat where a plant or animal normally lives

illegal against the law

pioneers the first people to live in a new area

poacher a person who hunts or fishes illegally

population the total number of a kind of animal living in a place

tagging putting a label on an animal in order to be able to identify it later

threatened to be in danger of dying out

track to follow an animal's movements

tranquilizer a drug that calms an animal or puts it to sleep

INDEX

READ MORE

Kenney, Karen Latchana. *Saving the Grizzly Bear (Great Animal Comebacks)*. Minneapolis: Jump! Inc. 2019.

Levy, Janey. *Grizzly Bears Bite! (Deadly Biters)*. New York: Gareth Stevens Publishing, 2021.

Murray, Julie. *Grizzly Bears (Animal Kingdom)*. Minneapolis: Abdo Publishing, 2020.

LEARN MORE ONLINE

1. Go to **www.factsurfer.com**
2. Enter **"Bear Comeback"** into the search box.
3. Click on the cover of this book to see a list of websites.